I Never Knew You

RD "Doc" Franklin

CONTENTS

ABOUT THE AUTHOR

R.D. Franklin is a 74 year old retiree, having spent his career as a building contractor. Self- employed for nearly fifty years. Much of that time has also been dedicated to studying the scriptures. He was married to his beautiful wife Sharon for fifty four years. She passed away from Covid-19 in September 2021. They had three children, Lisa, Angela, and Michael. He was given the nickname "Doc" by his friend John Jones because according to him, "Doc" can fix anything or solve any problem.

INTRODUCTION

"Not everyone who says to me Lord, Lord, will enter the kingdom of heaven, but only he who does the will of my father who is in heaven. Many will say to me on that day Lord, Lord, did we not prophesy in your name, and in your name drive out demons and preform many miracles? Then I will tell them plainly, "I NEVER KNEW YOU. Away from me, you evildoers." Matt. 7:21-23

Have you ever been scared? I'm not talking about being scared on that wild ride at the fair. Nor even the sort of scared you feel if someone jumps out at you in the dark. I'm talking SCARED! Those verses in Matthew are really scary! The casual reader, and yes even the "Christian" most often are not scared by those verses. But the Truth Seeker will be frozen in his spiritual tracks. "I NEVER KNEW YOU"... The Lord says He's talking plainly! If this doesn't scare you or concern you, then nothing further will either.

Chapter 1

A Voice Calling

"The heavens declare the glory of God; the skies proclaim the work of His hands" Psalm 19:1 "Fear not, for I have redeemed you; I have summoned you by name" Isaiah 43:1

It's early Sept. 1953, the sage grass (as we called it) was thick and tall. At least tall to a young boy of six Oh, the fun and good times we had, my siblings and I, in that field behind the old home place. A place my grandfather had built some twenty years earlier. Looking back the real fun most often was just lying in the sage grass, watching the clouds move in the sky, being at peace and enjoying the world around me.

"Duane" someone called! Raising up to look toward the house, expecting to see my mother on the back porch, I saw no one. Having looked circumspectly, shrugged my shoulders and lay back down. Enjoying the moment, for I knew later in the day it would be time for school. Yes, later in the day! It was the baby boom years, schools were very crowded. My first grade class was so large we went in shifts, half in the morning and half in the afternoon. I loved my mornings in the field.

"Duane" came the call! This time there was a more urgent tone, "dad" I thought? Again I could see no one. But being a child that strove to be obedient. And knowing when your name is called your presence is required, I ran to the house. Upon learning no one had called. I returned to my place in the field. Looking around and up at the sky, my thoughts turned to God.

I dared not ask aloud "is that you God? But silently pondered; if it was God then surely my presence was required. These thoughts troubled me; if I was called to where did I report, and how? What was the way to God?

Sunday school was fun, we learned Bible stories and made lots of neat crafts. I enjoyed the little church that sat not far from my field. But where was God?

Not long after my experience with a voice calling, I began to have dreams. We've all had dreams and some people experience recurring dreams. Permit me to share two recurring dreams, (1) in my field of sage grass I find a large white rock. After much digging it is discovered, the rock covers a cave entrance. To my surprise and great joy, the cavern is filled with rubies, diamonds, emeralds, gold and silver coins! (2) I find myself clinging to an old high top shoe, high above the ground. It seems to be thousands of feet.

Looking up the shoe lace disappears in the clouds. Who or what is holding it I don't know. These dreams came very frequently, sometimes both on the same night. Sometimes alternating but almost always both in one week. This in its self is amazing. But what is really amazing they continued for twenty seven years!

Let me pause here and say that the rest of this chapter or the rest of this book, may or may not be as personal. But my intent in writing at all is to share Christ: to be a witness. As we all know a witness can only attest to what he or she has seen or heard. I do not think that everyone must experience the things I share. But if a nugget of truth is gleaned, God be praised! I'm called to witness.

I spent years digging up that field, leaving not a stone unturned. After time the search for treasure was not so intense. But I knew there was something special about that field, about that spot.

As good boys go, I was a good boy. By the time I was fourteen or fifteen, the world held a strong attraction. Soon enticed and drawn by that magnetic like force, known as sin.

Lusting after all those selfish things in life. Oh, I always had that God given compassion, a big heart but deep down self-came first. Getting into everything imaginable, up to and including dealing drugs. Really if you can imagine it I more than likely did it.

The Lord is really patient and long suffering. He dealt with me lovingly, gently for twenty seven years. At the age of thirty three, after a sometimes stormy existence, I gave my life to Jesus. From that point in time the recurring dreams ceased. My life at times still seems like a stormy existence but I know who holds it!

As a young adult I was thrilled when my grandfather gave me that field. How wonderful I thought, I'll build a house here on this special spot. Alas a house was never built there. In fact the property was lost through a shady real estate deal. To this day I still drive by to look at my field. A special spot? Yes! The Lord was there, that's where I encountered God!

It wasn't until after my conversion, I realized what the Lord was trying to convey all those years. "My son, if you accept my words and store up my commands within you, turn your ear to wisdom and applying your heart to understanding. and if you call out for insight and cry aloud for understanding, and if you look for it as for silver and reach for it as for hidden treasure, then you will understand the fear of the Lord and find the knowledge of God" Pr. 2:1-5

"The kingdom of heaven is like treasure hidden in a field, when a man found it he hid it again, and in his joy went and sold all he had and bought that field". *Matt. 13:44*

These things I learned when one day, I said aloud "is that you God? If it is take my life Lord, I've messed it up, your way has got to be better!

My grandfather was a strong man, a man of character, a man that loved me! His love was not lost for I loved him and saw in him security. Even at a distance I knew my "Pap" by the clothes he wore. His shoes were what we called "high top" shoes.

So as I saw it the dream about clinging to an old high top shoe, was a symbol of my security.

Learning that the real GRAND Father: He who is shod in Truth and indeed is Truth! Knowing that He who holds all things holds my life!

As we proceed on our journey to understanding Matthew 7:21-23, let's not forget "Many are called but few are chosen". Matt.22:14

Oh Father God: the Ancient of Days, out of thy Holy Place Thou called me by name, and sought to teach me Thy ways; Lord teach me to pray and to speak Thy praise!

Chapter II

Faith

"Now faith is being sure of what we hope for and certain of what we do not see" Heb.11:1

Webster's tells us that faith-is confidence or trust in a person or thing. Strong's Exhaustive Concordance says-that every time the word faith is used in the Bible it is *trust i.e.* credence. Emunah (em-oo-naw) in Hebrew and Pistis (pis-tis) in the Greek. Few bible students have trouble with this-it's cut and dry, right? Well yes; but the problem is lots of folks equate faith with belief. Some will say whoa! Hold the phone, faith and belief do equate. Webster's again tells us that belief-is something believed, conviction, confidence, and trust! The real confusion lies in the fact that most people use the word faith to mean I will believe. In other words, to think it so, that is to work it up in one's mind.

It's what I call the "Peter Pan syndrome". Peter told the children "if you believe real hard you can fly". Have you ever heard a pastor or church official say "we're going to add a new wing, we'll just step out in faith"? Doesn't the scriptures say "being sure", certain? Where is the credence?

Can we make plans, then expect God to bless them or make them come to pass? The scriptures also tell us to say "if the Lord will" we will do such and such. We must be in the will of God.

There is the faith-trust we have in God: to take care of us, to do the things He promised in His word. He said "I will never leave you or forsake you", so we put our trust in Him.

We trust Him as a child trust a parent. What father has not set a child on a counter or table? Extended their arms and said jump. Almost always the child jumps without any hesitation. Why? Because the child trust dad will catch him. The child knows the father, knows that he loves him and will not harm him. In like manner as a child of God; we moment by moment trust Father. Knowing whatever comes our way has first been filtered through His hands of love. The word says "I know in whom I have believed" also "the just shall live by faith", that moment by moment trusting. As my beloved pastor (Howard Field) often said "all matters are in His hands".

Then there is the "faith" that lots of folks toss around and use I think in a wrong sense. It has been said that "if the lame just had enough faith he could walk." "If those around him had unbelief it would cancel out faith." No wonder there is so much confusion. The kind of faith we want to discuss has been called miracle working faith. We often read an ad for a miracle service or healing service. Saying "come get your miracle", some do. Most often though honest seekers will say, "I didn't have enough faith" or "I just couldn't believe hard enough."(The Peter Pan syndrome)

The Lord said "if you have faith as small as a mustard seed, you can say to this mountain, move from here to there and it will move, nothing will be impossible for you." Romans 12:3 tells us "God has dealt to every man the measure of faith." So we have faith! God has dealt us the measure. Given us the capacity, if you will, to trust, have faith. Why is the mountain not moved? Why is this thing we want changed not changed?

Let's question this a little further. In Matt. 21:21-22 "Jesus replied, I tell you the truth, if you have faith and do not doubt, not only can you do what was done to the fig tree, but also you can say to this mountain, go throw yourself into the sea; and it will be done. If you believe, you will receive whatever you ask for in prayer." Do we apply the Peter Pan syndrome? Look at the story of Jesus walking on the water. In Matt. 14 Jesus said "Take courage; it is I. don't be afraid." "Lord, if it's you" Peter (not Pan) replied, "Tell me to come to you on the water." "Come," He said. (Notice Peter didn't say, Hey! He's walking on water, I believe I can do that, I'll just step out on faith.") Then Peter got down out of the boat, walked on the water and came toward Jesus. But when he saw the wind, he was afraid and beginning to sink, cried out "Lord save me! Immediately Jesus reached out His hand and caught him. "You of little faith, He said why did you doubt?" First of all, Peter cried out "Lord if it's you" and he believed it was. He said "tell me to come to you on the water." I like the way the King James reads, "bid me come" Secondly, he got out of the boat and walked on the water; acted on what he heard.

Remember when Peter and the others went fishing? The Lord told them "launch out into the deep and let down your net." They had fished all night and caught nothing but said…"never the less at thy word I will let down the net." Do you see what is going on? Simon Peter said… "At thy word." There was the royal official with a sick child, who begged Jesus to heal him, Jesus replied, "You may go. Your son will live. The man took Jesus at His word and departed."

David, Jehoshaphat and Hezekiah kings of Judah, they trusted in the Lord. When an enemy approached, they did not say, the Lord has been with us in past battles. He will be with us now and bring victory. NO! They inquired of the Lord saying "shall we go up against them?" When He said "go" at His word they went up in faith! It's been said, "Faith is not the frantic clutching at a desperate hope. Rather faith is an application of heavenly power to a situation which we are assured will thereby be changed." How are we assured? WE HEAR FROM GOD! The word says "today if you hear His voice harden not your heart." Know who is speaking to you, believe and act on what you hear. That's saving faith! The Lord says "my sheep know my voice." The bible teaches us that there are many voices in this world and we are to try the spirits and see if they be of God. The Lord will confirm His word. He will witness to our spirit. As we desire the Lord and walk with Him, His voice becomes more familiar.

We've all heard someone say "the Lord told me." When we hear this kind of talk we generally receive it in one of two ways; 1) We believe them to be some kind of nut. 2) Our spiritual ears perk up and listen for the witness of the Spirit.

You know, church folks are the worst, they worship and pray to God. With all sorts of requests, never expecting Him to say anything. They even tell you He has said all He's going to say, in His printed word, the Bible. I confirm He will not say anything contrary to the Bible. He does speak to, guide and direct His children.

Matthew tells us in chapter 18:19-20 "Again, I tell you that if two of you on earth agree about anything you ask for, it will be done for you by my Father in heaven. For where two or three come together in my name, there am I with them." The King James says "there am I in the midst of them." Are the scriptures true? Why aren't these things happening? As we read this you would think that two or three of us could decide to clear the hospital beds, if we so agreed. The Lord said "There am I in the midst." He is not to be ignored, He wants us to agree with Him, NOT amongst ourselves. We can't force God to act just because we say He must.

Even if we quote Him scripture, as the manner of some is.

When God speaks and we answer in obedience, resurrection power comes into play! His will is accomplished.

Permit me to share somethings the Lord has done. As a young Christian I felt that obedience was foremost with being in Gods will, I still do. When God speaks we are required to act! One day while grocery shopping with my small children; we saw a man selling pencils in front of the store. My oldest daughter said "look daddy, that man is blind." "Yes" I replied, as we acquired a shopping cart and began to stroll through the store. "Pray for him" I heard the Lord say. "I will" I answered "I will." "Pray for him NOW!" the spirit said. "But Lord, he doesn't even have eyeballs!" I argued. "Pray" He said. Obediently I went, my mind racing, what was I to say? What was I to do? Nervously I approached him and asked if he knew Jesus, he said "Yes." "How long have you been blind" I asked? "All my life he said. "Do you mind if I pray for you? "No, please do" he replied. So there on the sidewalk, I began to pray for him. He thanked me. My children and I left.

On the drive home I began to be upset, because the man's eyes were not restored. Questioning God; "Why did you have me pray if you were not going to heal him?" Later as I pondered this the Lord spoke to my heart, "you were obedient." That's been many years ago. The man hasn't been seen since. Before he was there almost every day, for years don't know if "Praise God" he was healed or just left town. Maybe he died, I don't know. The Lord has not allowed me to be privy to that.

Another time as I was taking out the trash. One of the garbage men asked, "Do you know anybody that can remove warts?" Assuming he was asking about a "wart witch," (you know one of those people who claim to have power to remove warts) And wanting no part of that, said "no I don't know anyone that does that."

I felt sorry for him, he had large warts all over his hand, front and back. Some were bleeding where he had bumped and scraped them.

After exchanging stories and other small talk he walked back to his truck. Turning toward my house, "So you don't know anyone that can remove warts" spoke the Lord? Knowing immediately what I must do what had to be done. Calling to him as he emerged from the truck, at the next house.

Moving toward him. Imagining laying hands on him and praying in the name of Jesus! As he looked up, "it turns out I do know someone who Can remove warts" I said. "Who" he asked? "The Lord God" I exclaimed! "I know that" he groaned. Sticking my finger in his face "trust Him and they'll vanish"! "Ok" he said, climbing into his truck and driving off.

Why did I say that? Why did I do that? Nothing went the way it was imagined. Knowing in my heart God was in it, I walked back to the house.

Trash pick-up is every Friday morning. Being out of town the next Friday; I missed him. But the following trash day was different. Standing in the driveway, leaning against my truck, watching as he emptied trash cans. "Lord, it doesn't look good for the home team, he hasn't said a word." "Hey" I yelled "How's the warts?" With this he threw down the trash can and ran at me! "Whoa" I thought, what's wrong? As he drew near me jerked off his glove, sticking his hand in my face said "They're gone!" "Praise the Lord" I yelled as we both rejoiced!

Years ago my mother in-law had been diagnosed with stomach cancer. Through surgery it was discovered the cancer was massive and inoperable. She knew she had cancer but was not told the extent of it. (A family decision) WE were told she had about three months. To comfort her the doctors prescribed morphine, with which she injected herself at will.

One day a stranger came to the door and asked if anyone was sick? My mother in-law began to tell of her cancer. The stranger, a woman, said "I was driving down the street, when the Lord told me to stop and pray for someone in this house who is sick." After praying for healing, the woman left. She hasn't been seen since. When three months had come and gone, the doctors could not find the cancer! To God's glory she lived more than twenty years!

What am I saying? "Faith comes by hearing and hearing by the word of God"! Whether our first encounter with God is a voice calling audibly or a spiritual whisper to your heart. As the word says "We must come to God believing that He is, and is the rewarder of those who diligently seek Him." Dear one do you diligently seek Him? "You will seek me and find me when you seek me with all your heart. I will be found of you" declares the Lord. Jer. 29:13

When He speaks we must answer and we must answer with deep felt trust in Him who holds all things. Knowing He is the rewarder of those that diligently seek Him. Desiring above all things a deep personal relationship, with the creator of the universe. Not settling for an impersonal *churchy* relationship with a god whom we perceive to be mute. But a real relationship of communication. A real partaking of the Lord Jesus, a Holy Communion, if you will.

"Thou hast called and I did answer.

Bind thou me as I cleave to thee, hold my
hand that
I may not stumble,

Make me thy man and keep me humble!"

Chapter III

Repentance

"Repent and be baptized, every one of you in the name of Jesus Christ for the forgiveness of your sins. And you will receive the gift of the Holy Spirit." Acts 2:38

What does it mean to repent? How does one repent? Is repentance really necessary? Let's discuss these questions and more as we journey to understand Matt. 7:1-23

It's been said "to repent is to be sorry." That is certainly part of it, for the Word says "Godly sorrow leads to repentance." But it is much deeper than that! For it also has been said "to repent is to change one's mind." Webster's tells us much the same thing. It says repent means 1) to feel contrite (for), regret. 2) To be penitent (for) and determine to change for the better. Repent in the Greek is metanoeo, to think differently, i.e. reconsider. The Greek for repentance is metanoia, reversal of decision.

Dr. William Chamberlain wrote, "Repentance is change of mind. A change of mind from the selfish human outlook, to the self-giving mind of Christ leads to abundant living." George Campbell said "everyone who reforms repents, but everyone who repents does not reform." So then repentance is more than sorry, more than change of mind, but change of mind with change of conduct.

As a man thinkest in his heart so is he" Esau was tearfully sorry and ashamed that he had sold his birthright. Sorry that his brother Jacob received the blessing. You see his desires and his appetites controlled him. He treated his birthright as a flippant thing. The Word says "He could bring about no change of mind (repentance) though he sought the blessing with tears." referencing Heb. 12:17 Dr. Chamberlain said "Esau was a man weeping and protesting over the loss of a blessing caused by his own appetites, but with those appetites unchanged; so, had opportunity offered again, the birthright might have been sold again for physical gratification."

What of Judas? Scripture tells us he "repented himself and brought again the thirty pieces of silver to the chief priest and elders; saying I have sinned in that I have betrayed innocent blood"… "And went and hanged himself." Did he repent? His repentance was that of sorry, not of reform: a changed life. It was a repentance of shame, thus instead of a change of life, he took his life.

Keith Green of Last Days Ministries, who was killed in a plane crash several years ago, often said "repentance must gush forth" Second Timothy tells us "…gently instruct, in the hope that God will grant them repentance, leading them to a knowledge of truth." Did you hear that? "…God will grant them repentance." Does that mean it is up to God whether or not we repent? That's a whole other book, but yes; repentance is a prerequisite for salvation. It is by Grace we are saved, not of ourselves. This is a great mystery but it is the work of God, may He be praised forever more! Therefore repentance as Keith Green said "must gush forth" not of ourselves but the power of God working in us.

In my own conversion experience, I had come to a point in life a change absolutely had to take place. With my mind set on Christ, my conduct conformed (as best I could), I slipped to the alter. Long after the alter call, so long in fact, no one knew I was there. Reasoning, those folks assumed my good standing in the church. This was a shame factor... not wanting to be seen kneeling at the alter. Knowing all that was required for salvation was believing and saying a prayer.

My wife and I were attending a James Roberson crusade. He brought a wonderful message. When the invitation came, I was drawn like a magnet to the front of the stage. Nearing the stage all control was lost, fell on my face, began to weep and sob uncontrollably. Sobbing so hard my whole body started to convulse. I could not stop sobbing and shaking, though I greatly desired to. It was as if my inner being, my spirit was broken and separate from my flesh, mournful. After what seemed like an eternity, I was able to stand and compose myself; feeling weak yet somehow renewed.

"This is the one I esteem; he who is humble and contrite in spirit trembles at my word." Isaiah 66:2 Contrite, an interesting word. As used in this scripture, the Hebrew word is Nakeh (naw-keh) it means = smitten, i.e. (lit.) maimed, wounded. "For this is what the High and Lofty One says, He who lives forever, whose name is Holy: I live in a high and holy place, but also with him who is contrite and lowly in spirit, to revive the spirit of the lowly and to revive the heart of the contrite." Isaiah 57:15 Here in this verse the Hebrew word is daka (daw-kaw) = a crushed spirit. "The sacrifices of God are a broken spirit; a broken and contrite heart, O God, you will not despise." Ps. 51:17 Again the Hebrew word for contrite is dakah (dak-kaw) to collapse (phys. or mentally)

What a shame lots of folks fall (literally into hell) for this easy believism. As we know "the angels of hell believe and tremble." Thank God this was not the case. Having acknowledged Jesus and His redemptive work on the cross, turned to Him from my sinful ways and confessed the need of a savior. But after several days I knew something was not quite right.

"The Lord is close to the brokenhearted and saves those who are crushed in spirit." Psalm 34:18 (contrite)

This time the Hebrew word is dakka (dak-kaw) crushed spirit, as powder.

"Create in me a clean heart, O God; and renew a right spirit within me." Psalm 51:10 it is all the Lord's doing. "Know ye that the Lord He is God: it is He that hath made us, and not we ourselves"

Ps. 100:3 It is by His Grace (unmerited favor) that we are able to repent. Our spirit being fast bound in sin, cannot save itself. Moreover will not call on God, it is God that calls and awakens this sleeping being. Putting us in a position to receive Him. Like the last stanza in one of my favorite hymns; "Long my imprisoned spirit lay, fast bound in sin and nature's night. Thine eyes diffused a quickening ray- I woke, the dungeon flamed with light; my chains fell off, my heart was free, I rose, went forth, and followed Thee.

Grace what a wonderful word, the Old Testament uses the Hebrew word - chen (khane) =kindness, favor. Two root words, one being; chanah, to incline, or to pitch as a tent, "Lot... pitched his tent toward Sodom)" The word chanah by impl. To decline (of the slanting rays of evening). The other root word is chanan =meaning to bend or stoop in kindness to an inferior. The New Testament uses the Greek word charis (khar'ece) meaning graciousness, the divine influence upon the heart, and it's reflection in life...

It's by His Grace we are saved. Dear one can you see the Creator of the universe bending down to deliver a divine call; a spiritual whisper to your heart? Better yet can you hear? That is Grace in the ultimate sense. Remember the scripture? That says; "No man can come to me, except the Father which hath sent me draw him, and I will raise him up at the last day. It is written in the prophets, and they shall be all taught of God. Every man therefore that hath heard, and hath learned of the Father, cometh unto me." John 6:44-45

So we are able to repent when drawn, i.e. called again "Many are called but few are chosen." Are you called? Has that quickening ray sparked a flame in your soul? Is it a flame that lights the way to a different path, a path that leads to a changed mind, a reformed life? Dear one do you hunger and thirst after righteousness? Do you know forgiveness?

Chapter IV

Forgiveness

"If thou, Lord, shouldest mark iniquities, O Lord who shall stand? But there is forgiveness with thee, that thou mayest be feared." Psalm 130:3-4

Forgiveness as defined in scripture is freedom, pardon, liberty. The word forgive in the Greek is *aphiemi*, meaning to send forth, lay aside, put away. The root word is *apelauno*, to dismiss.

I know you are probably getting tired of these word definitions, Can't say I blame you. On the other hand it is very important to understand what is being said, especially as words are used in scripture.

Gerald Ford pardoned Richard Nixon, as president he had that authority. Forgiveness or pardon can be obtained from or given by one who has authority to do so. In the story of the paralytic of Mark 2:5-11; Jesus said "Son, your sins are forgiven." "Now some teachers of the law were sitting there, thinking to themselves, "Why does this fellow talk like that? He's blaspheming! Who can forgive sins but God alone?" Immediately Jesus knew in His spirit that this was what they were thinking in their hearts, and He said to them, "Why are you thinking these things? Which is easier: to say to the paralytic, your sins are forgiven or to say, get up take your mat and walk? But that you may know that the Son of Man has authority on earth to forgive sins..."He said to the paralytic, I tell you, get up, take your mat and go home."

Jesus said..."Which is easier: to say...your sins are forgiven or to say, Get up....? Being healed and being forgiven are very synonymous; but hold that thought we'll discuss it later.

The Lord certainly has the authority to forgive sins. The Word tells us..."If we confess our sins, He is faithful and just to forgive us our sins, and to cleanse us from all unrighteousness."..." And He is the propitiation..." Propitiation, now there's a big word, just what does it mean? First it means = atonement. In both the Greek and Hebrew = to make amends, to make different; to change, to restore, also the root meaning is to pitch, to put away. Much like the word forgiveness. So we can say The Lord is forgiveness, and in Him we have forgiveness. "Abide in me, and I in you..."If a man abide not in me, he is cast forth as a branch, and is withered, and men gather them, and cast them into the fire, and they are burned."

Why forgiveness? In a word "sin". But what is sin? Well..."sin is the transgression of the law" 1 John 3:4. Some will say we are not under the law but under grace. Indeed we are and if you remember we touched on "Grace" in chapter three. Romans 6:1 tells us "What shall we say then? Shall we continue in sin, that grace may abound? God forbid. How shall we that are dead to sin, live any longer therein?"

Let us address this sin question. H.V. Miller stated in his book "The Sin Problem" "The sin question is the pivotal question. Anything taught or preached which obscures the curciality of sin becomes an enemy of the Cross of Christ." Sin and our concept of it is most serious. For if we have a wrong view or notion of sin, we could very well miss the Kingdom. You see the base meaning of the word sin is to miss the mark. (And so not share in the prize) see chapter 7)

Say a pilot was flying a plane from Knoxville, TN. to Las Vegas, NV. Suppose he got off course one tenth of one degree, where might he wind up? Actually, it would depend at what point he got off course. Assuming he got off at the point of origin, then he would be approximately five miles north or south of Las Vegas; depending which way he turned. Point being, a very small step from the narrow way, plunges one in to the abyss. Put another way, any exit from the narrow way becomes *the Broad Way.* " Enter ye at the strait gate: for wide is the gate, and broad is the way, that leadeth to destruction, and many there be which go in thereat: because strait is the gate, and narrow is the way, which leadeth unto life, and few there be that find it." My I strongly remind you of the very next sentence of scripture. Matt. 7:15 "Watch out for false prophets..."

As stated before "Anything taught or preached which obscures the cruciality of sin becomes an enemy of the Cross of Christ." Dear one a miss is a miss, as the old saying goes "to miss it an inch is to miss it a mile." If we miss the mark we sin, and if we sin we need forgiveness. Thank God forgiveness comes through Christ Jesus and His shed Blood; making the way of salvation. By His righteousness overcame unrighteousness, and by His death made it possible for us to have victory over sin. Let us say with Paul..."I press toward the mark for the prize of the high calling of God in Christ Jesus."

"Let us therefore, as many as be perfect (mature), be thus minded, God shall reveal even this unto you. Nevertheless, to the degree that we have already attained, let us walk by the same rule, let us be of the same mind." Phil. 3:15-16

Having sinned, having missed the mark, we need our sin put away, dismissed, pardoned. Why, because it feels good? Yes: forgiveness or being forgiven tends to make one feel good. But more important, forgiveness does away with the penalty of sin. Isn't that great? How can one whose charges have been dismissed be held accountable? Truth is he can't; unless of course he again becomes a law breaker. Sin and its penalty can be dismissed. But the results of wrong doing, transgression, and "sin" are irreversible.

Suppose a child angrily broke a vase. Later repents and receives forgiveness, pardon: The vase is still broken. Parents or others must bear the expense. Another example: if one man killed the other, was sent to prison and later received a pardon. Guess what? The victim is still dead. Put another way, while in prison the killer finds forgiveness through Jesus, is free of guilt perhaps and is at peace with God: You got it! He is still in prison; the victim still dead, the family and loved ones of both the prisoner and the victim still grieve. Almost always these loved ones feel guilt, anger, hate or bitterness: that is carried by them, leveled at others and passed on to others, the end of which is unimaginable!

Before we go on allow me to interject a thought. The punishment of God's laws and the punishment of man's laws are not the same. Even though they may intersect or overlap, and God may use man's punishment to discipline. I.e. The killer is, through forgiveness free of God's punishment for murder, but is in prison fulfilling man's law.

As stated earlier, being healed and being forgiven are very synonymous. The fact being, to be forgiven is to be free from that which binds. Sin has us bound, through sin came sickness and disease. The scripture says "by His wounds you have been healed" 1 Peter 2:21 Healed of what? Praise God, sin!

Chances are you've heard the phrase, "The sins of the father?" If you will indulge, let me quote a few verses of scripture. "...and he (Abijam) walked in all the sins of his father, which he had done before him: and his heart was not perfect with the Lord his God..." 1 Kings 15:3 "... forgiving iniquity and transgression and sin, that will by no means clear the guilty; visiting the iniquity of the fathers upon the children, and upon the children's children, unto the third and to the fourth generation." Ex. 34:7

In this next scripture Jesus is speaking of The Father, but pay close attention to what is said. "Verily, verily, I say unto you, The Son can do nothing of himself, but what he seeth the Father do: for what things soever he doeth, these also doeth the Son likewise." Children are very easily influenced by others especially parents, and more particularly the father. A child's relationship with the father is the most important relationship of their life. Because it is the basis for all other relationships.

We hear a lot these days about genetics. About how some of us are predisposed to this disease or that behavior. Well some things are genetic, like hair or eye color, and yes some sicknesses are passed from father to child. The most devastating is sin. In the truest sense sin is both inherent and inherited. (Don't lose that thought, we'll discuss it more later.)

There was an article in the newspaper awhile back that said: "Scientists Seek Inherited Genetic Link to Alcoholism". The article read in part: "...Researchers strongly suspect the risk of becoming an alcoholic can be inherited, a genetic predisposition that may be passed from father to son." The article went on to ask "...Is behavior picked up like childhood toys, and learned from the environment around us or is it inherited?"

Friend, we may have a genetic predisposition to this or that. We can even have a genetic link to our "bent". (As a twig is bent, so grows the tree) Are we not our father's child? The media has pushed hard the modern idea that homosexuality is in the genes, it's not their fault, they're made that way. If this is true, the Word of God is a lie. Praise the Lord, we know better! How can God command obedience if we are incapable of compliance? Listen very carefully, behavior is a matter of the will. The Bible, especially the book of Colossians, reminds me of a Nike commercial, "Just do it". Do what He commands, do what is right!

Jesus speaks of doing those things He sees the Father do. Likewise children are the same way, they mimic dad. They try to walk like dad, and do all sorts of things to be like daddy. The younger the child the more like dad they try to be. That is before the world and all of its deception has flooded their lives.

To a child their father is "it", he can do no wrong. Even when the father does wrong, the child will often reason otherwise. Sometimes even when a child knows dad has done wrong, his mind will tell him, this is dad and if dad is doing it, it somehow has got to be right.

Take the issue of alcoholism. The newspaper article previously mentioned stated: "Research has shown there is a strong connection between chronic drinking and the alcoholic's family history." The connection is not genetic as some would say. I say there's a link alright, a demonic link! It's more than a child following the father's example. Why is this problem so difficult, so seemingly binding?

The Word tells "If your brother sins against you, go and show him his fault, just between the two of you…" Matt. 18:15. You know the story: if he listens, you've won your brother over. But if not, take witnesses, if he still doesn't listen, you go to the church. Matthew 18:17 says: "I tell you the truth, whatever you bind on earth will be bound in heaven, and whatever you loose on earth will be loosed in heaven."

Following in the same chapter 18 of Matt. The story is told of a king who was settling accounts. It was found that one servant owed a great amount, and unable to pay. The king took pity on him and forgave the debt. The King James reads, "Then the lord of that servant was moved with compassion, and loosed him and forgave him the debt." His problems had him bound, the one to whom he was a problem had the authority to loose him through forgiveness.

Stephen, as he was being stoned, "...cried with a loud voice, Lord, lay not this sin to their charge!" Acts 7:60 John 20:23 says "If you forgive anyone his sins, they are forgiven: if you do not forgive them, they are not forgiven."

Dr. Cole told a story, I think it was in his book, "Maximized Manhood." That book is not in my possession, so I'll relate the story as best I can. After speaking to a group, a man and woman approached Dr. Cole and asked him to pray for their son, who was an alcoholic. The Dr. said he would be glad to, but first would ask the man a question. "Have you ever been an alcoholic?" "Well yes" the man said. But that was a long time ago." Questioning further "Were you a drunk in the home, in front of the boy as he was growing up?" "Yes" the man said. "Has he ever forgave you" quizzed Dr. Cole? "I'm sure he has" replied the man. "That's not what I asked you" "Has he personally forgiven you" asked the Dr.? "Well no" "I tell you what, go ask your son to forgive you, then we'll pray" replied the kind Dr.

The man went to his son, asked his forgiveness. After a few months the son received Christ and quit drinking. (My apologies to Dr. Cole, he told the story much better) Years ago after reading Dr. Cole's book, I realized or began to realize, the impact forgiveness has in one's life. Admittedly being forgiven is something we want, in fact need. If for nothing else to feel better about ourselves. But to understand forgiveness can loose the ties that bind; was a wonderful revelation.

Expecting he would defend himself, he just lowered his head in shame. "I truly forgive you it's alright dad" as we embraced. My father I'm sure felt some relief, a lifted weight perhaps. But I was free! The sins of my father were not bound to me. Nor were they laid to his charge.

Going immediately to my mother; "Mom" "forgive me for not being the son I should have." she did. "Mom I forgive you for not being the mother you should have." I was on a roll and feeling great!

AS previously stated, "sin is both inherent and inherited." So, for understanding and clarity-inherited of course means: to have received as an heir, from predecessors or to have received (a genetic character) by heredity. Inherent means existing in someone or something as a permanent and inseparable quality or attribute. Sin (the curse of) certainly is passed from father to child (i.e. the blood), and sin is that which tends to be permanent and inseparable (without The Blood).

The Word tells us "the life is in the blood" also abideth death. Jesus said "I am come that they might have life, and that they might have it more abundantly." The sin that Adam bound to himself, brought death to all his unborn children. We as children ratify this by our own acts of sin. Having an inherited- inherent "sin nature" we continue to sin. Being fast bound and without hope. "It is appointed unto man once to die, but after this the Judgment." We will die but as to what comes after, is by our own acts of sin.

My father came to mind as I pondered the "Binding and loosing" theology. Forgive, I must forgive my father! "Ok, but how to approach dad? He was a stern man. Not knowing how he would react and being somewhat fearful, yet boldly determined. I went to see him.

He was sitting in his easy chair, reading a book. Which was how he spent most of his time. It had been said "He's read most everything in print." (Unfortunately, don't think he read much of the Bible.) Dad had an IQ around 180, I loved to pick his brain, and he had vast stores of knowledge. But today something more urgent was pressing. Nearing his chair, I got down on one knee beside him. "Got a second dad?" "Yeah" he answered. Expressing how I had not been the son that I should have. That his forgiveness was needed. "Will you forgive me dad? "Sure son" he said. "And dad; I want to forgive you for not being the father you should have." "For being an alcoholic" His head lowered with each thing I said.

Expecting he would defend himself, he just lowered his head in shame.

"I truly forgive you, it's alright dad "as we embraced. My father, I'm sure felt some relief, a lifted weight perhaps. But I was free! The sins of my father were not bound to me. Nor were they laid to his charge.

Going immediately to my mother; "Mom, forgive me for not being the son I should have" she did. "Mom I forgive you for not being the mother you should have." I was on a roll and feeling great!

As previously stated, "sin is both inherent and inherited." So for understanding and clarity, inherited of course means: to have received as an heir, from predecessors or to have received (a genetic character) by heredity. Inherent means existing in someone or something as a permanent and inseparable quality or attribute. Sin (the curse of) certainly is passed from father to child, (i.e. the blood) and sin is that which tends to be permanent and inseparable. (without The Blood)

The Word tells us "the life is in the blood", also abideth death. Jesus said "I am come that they might have life, and that they might have it more abundantly." The sin that Adam bound to himself, brought death to all his unborn children. We as children ratify this by our own acts of sin. Having an inherited- inherent "sin nature" we continue to sin. Being fast bound and without hope. "It is appointed unto man once to die, but after this the Judgment," We will die but as to what comes after, by our own acts of sin.

Before I get ahead of myself, let me simply say: as Adam bound sin to himself, in like manner we also bind to ourselves sin and the sins of others. Forgiveness frees or loosens us from that which binds. Bring bound we will tend to

be hurt by that sin and repeat it. Our prayers are hindered, we lack the power of God, and our life is in shambles. So we must forgive those that do us hurt, that we not be bound by their sin. "For if you forgive men when they sin against you, your heavenly Father will also forgive you. But if you do not forgive men their sins, your Father will not forgive your sins." Matt. 6:14-15

"...Bless them that curse you, do good to them that hate you, and pray for them which despitefully use you, that ye may be the children of your Father..." Meditate on these scriptures as we continue our journey.

Chapter V

Be of This Attitude

The Beatitudes are said to be declarations of blessedness or happiness and well they are. His disciples came to Him and He began to teach them, saying, "Blessed are the poor in spirit: for theirs is the kingdom of heaven", Matt. 5:1, 2. Declarations? Yes, but more than that, He taught them. So let's focus on what Jesus was trying to convey.

First of all we need to understand the manner in which Jesus taught. Most often He used parables: parables being something brought along side to make a point or comparison. His teachings were mainly metaphysical and spiritual. With this in mind we can begin to understand; how Jesus used things in society and nature to bring His point home to the listener. On one hand making His point abundantly clear. On the other concealing it to the selfish, hardhearted and the unspiritual.

In the parable of the sower Jesus concludes with "He that has ears, let him hear." Matt. 13:9 He went on to say "Though seeing, they do not see; though hearing, they do not hear or understand." In this is the fulfillment of the prophecy of Isaiah: "You will be ever hearing but never understanding; you will be ever seeing but never perceiving. For this people's heart has become calloused; they hardly hear with their ears, and they have closed their eyes, Otherwise they might see with their eyes, hear with their ears, understand with their hearts and turn, and I would heal them." Matt. 13:13-15

Dear friend, one may understand an allegory or a metaphor, but only spirit can understand spiritual. Understand this: the Holy Spirit reveals things to a yielded spirit. Having said that, let me again quote Matt. 5:3 "Blessed are the poor in spirit; for theirs is the kingdom of heaven."

Thus far we have used a lot of word definitions. Why stop now, right? We can intellectualize (there's a good word) this verse on and on but pray for spiritual understanding.

We need not elaborate the word - blessed. Most of us can grasp the idea of blessed. The word poor as defined by Webster's is: having little or no money or means of support. That doesn't quite fit the context does it? Take a look at this word in the Greek as used in scripture. The word poor here is: Ptochos (pto-khos) and from the word ptosso (to crouch or to cringe) a beggar-beggarly. So we could say, blessed are the beggarly in spirit. Which would be saying one was begging for spirit. That is the right attitude, blessed is he that has come to a place where he realizes a need for spiritual renewal. Also a begging desire for the Holy Spirit. The overwhelming sense is that of servility. Stated in this deeper and more meaningful way would be: Blessed are the slavishly submissive in spirit; for theirs is the kingdom of heaven.

Saul (Paul) as he went toward Damascus, breathing out threatenings and slaughter against the disciples of the Lord, "...suddenly there shined round about him a light from heaven, and he fell to earth, and heard a voice saying unto him, SAUL, SAUL, why persecutest thou me? And he said, "Who art thou Lord?" And the Lord said,"I am Jesus whom thou persecutest: it is hard for thee to kick against the pricks." Pricks? What are pricks? The Amplified Bible reads-"... It is dangerous and turns out badly for you to keep kicking against the goad, that is' to offer vain and perilous resistance." A goad or prick is what we would call a cattle prod. It was a stick, more often a sharp stick used to drive or direct cattle. Oh, how we resist the prodding of God, how it turns out badly.

"Trembling and astonished he asked, Lord, "What do you desire me to do?" Acts 9:6 Saul, would you say was cringing and crouching? (Ptosso) He had moved into an attitude of servility. He had changed, in verse 5 Saul says "...Who are you lord?" Lord in this particular verse means Sir! Then in verse 6 he says "...Lord, what do you desire me to do? The word Lord here means master! See the change?

God is calling; extending Grace, bending down to man. Hearing the call we set out to respond. All the while goading us, driving prodding. Yet self resists prodding. Self knows the way! Oh, how we resist the prodding of God, how it turns out badly. The Word says "If any man will come after me, let him deny himself, and take up his cross, and follow me." Friend, would you come after Jesus? Are you driven to Him in fear of hell, or the reward of heaven?

Those things are often what brings about thoughts of God, Jesus, salvation. And sometimes the very thing that leads to salvation, but somewhere along the line we must submit. Salvation begins with real submission. One must deny himself, not in lip service, but truly surrender to the Great I Am. Trembling and quaking in His awesome presence! Loving Him because He loved us so much in giving Himself as a sacrifice. ("And Isaac said...where is the lamb for a burnt sacrifice? Abraham said, my son, God will provide Himself...")

See, we no longer just want to shun hell, or gain heaven. (That in and if itself, is selfish.) We must serve Him out of love. "Love seeks not its own." This surrender is unto death, death of self. And a dead man has no rights! Thus we could say happy is the submitted spirit, for his is the kingdom of heaven.

Self-desire is what fills most of our lives. The Lord wants us to desire Him: in love with our maker. This can only take place if we are surrendered. You say talk is cheap. How does one surrender? Simply quit fighting; quit resisting the prodding of God, quit fighting with yourself. Nothing imprisons the heart, the spirit more than a defeated warrior who will not surrender. Not knowing that even death would not end the turmoil. In the natural world one would think, and rightly so, that the conqueror would slay or worse, abuse the surrendering warrior.

Who would want to fall into hands of man? Mankind being totally depraved, is subject to be most cruel. But to place one's self in the nail scared hands of Him whom we have to do: One receives mercy, forgiveness and FREEDOM. Oh, freedom, riding above the ills and trials of life. Having surrendered, having died to self, to this life, to the cares of this world. There is no hold on one who has let go.

You can't kill one who has chosen to die. You can't break one who is broken (contrite). And one who wants nothing cannot be bribed. Thus life begins in death. And freedom comes with life: Life lived above the ills of this world.

Imagine, an angry sea; the waves rolling, surging, the sea rising and falling. In these waters are poor souls fighting to stay alive. What a horrifying scene. But wait! What's this, a surfer riding high atop the waves? This is an image of one who through self-denial has risen above the world.

This is great, hopefully we can begin to understand what the Lord requires. What has been said thus far, some might see as pharisaical piety. So let's take a look at what else our Lord had to say.

Chapter VI

A Bible Study

God said "Let us make man (flesh) in our image, after our likeness:" Gen. 1:26 *Elohim*-God and the sons of God. The Almighty, who had taken creature form in order to create. The created beings, *spirits*-angels if you will. Notice, that every place in the Old Testament, where the term *sons of God* is used, it is *angels.* (Job 1:6, 2:1, 38:7 Ps. 29:1, 89:6 Dan. 3:25 Gen. 6:2,4 and in Gen. 6:2 of the Septuagint renders it *angels.*)

"And it came to pass, when men began to multiply on the face of the earth, and daughters were born unto them, That the sons of God saw the daughters of men that they were fair; and they took them wives of all which they chose," Gen. 6:1,2 "There were giants in the earth in those days; and also after that, when the sons of God came in to the daughters of men, and they bare children to them, the same became mighty men which were of old, men of renown. Gen. 6:4 The term; men *of old,* translates-from the vanishing point-from eternity.

Many so-called bible scholars say that *sons of God* in Gen. 6 refers to the Godly line of Seth. Nothing could be farther from the truth. (Do they not want to know the truth?) So, did spirits (having come into this dimension) impregnate women? Let's look at Jude v.6 "And the angels which kept not their first estate, but left their own habitation, He hath reserved in everlasting chains under darkness unto the judgement of that great day." Jude 6 obviously speaks of fallen angels and the nature of their fall. "And the angels which kept not their first estate..." *estate* translated peri, pronounced - peree, literally their *own principality.* Think about that! "...But left their own *habitation*" this word in the Greek is oiketerion (oy-kay-tat'-ree-on) and occurs only one other time-in 2 Cor. 5:2-meaning the spiritual body.

These disobedient spirits or angels left, cut a trail, when God said "Let us make man..." They didn't want to be born of woman -they wanted to seduce woman! What, you may ask? Let's back-up a little to Genesis 3:15 where God said "And I will put enmity between thee and the woman, between thy seed and her Seed;" We know that this scripture is the first promise of a savior for mankind. That through woman would come The Savior. So in Ch. 4:1 Eve is saying "I have gotten a man from the Lord." She thought she had brought forth The Savior. However this was not the case. Satan intended to foil God's plan by corrupting the pedigree of mankind.

Back to ch.6 of Gen. in verse 9 "... Noah was a just man and perfect in his generations..." Not a perfect man but an uncorrupted blood line. The world had become corrupt through these fallen angels. Their offspring, called Nephilim (giants) were beings of iniquity and had to be destroyed. Thus the flood of Noah and the first influx or irruption of fallen angels. (of the "sons of God")

Satan in his attempt to make void the Word of God. Sent forth his minions to adulterate the pedigree (DNA) of mankind. Therefore the destruction of these beings was necessary.

When God chose Abraham, he and his decedents became the focus of attack. Notice Gen.12:6 When Abraham entered Canaan, the Canaanite was then in the land. Who were the Canaanites? Let's see, the Kenites (sons of Cain), Kenizzites, Kadmonites,

Hittites, Amorites, Perizzites, Girgashhites, Jebusites and the Rephaims. Rephaim sometimes is translated *the* dead *or* dead. Other descendants of the Nephilim were Anak and Rapha see Gen. 35:27 and Josh. 15:13, 21:11. This the 2nd *influx of the fallen ones.* The Lord told Israel to utterly destroy these people, though some escaped, hmmm.

The Lord God anointed David king over Israel. Guess who met David in the valley of Elah? Yeah, that's right, Goliath *the giant.* "...And he (David) took his staff in his hand, and chose him five smooth stones out of the brook..." 1 Samuel 17:40. You see Goliath had four brothers, just a thought.

The evil one now knew the Seed of woman would come by David's line. The Seed royal was under attack. We could document centuries of these assaults but let's not. I feel we're being too detailed as it is. The intent is to convey lots of information without too much verbiage. Bear with me all roads lead somewhere.

When "the Seed of woman" Himself came, all hell was thrown at Him. His mother could have been stoned, Herod, the storms finally the cross. "Up from the grave He arose with a mighty triumph o'er His foes." I love that song!

Ok, we've been discussing these Nephilim, hybrids if you will. They (the procreate (fathers) were "sons of God" created spirit beings from "the fall." Let's review some scripture. "As it is written, Jacob have I loved, but Esau have I hated." Rom. 9:13 Hated? That's a strong word, *miseo* in the Greek, meaning: to detest, or persecute). What do we make of that? How about Jeremiah 1:5 "Before I formed thee in the belly I knew thee; and before thou camest forth out of the womb I sanctified thee...". This infers prior knowledge, the word *knew* in Hebrew is yada *-yaw-dah,* meaning to know (to ascertain by seeing). Look at John 9:2 "And His disciples asked Him, saying Master, who did sin, this man, or his parents, that he was born blind?" What do you think when you read this? I've read volumes on this scripture but none asks the question that jumps out at me. PRENATAL SIN? Sure his parents could have sinned and I'm sure they did. But "this man" sinned prior to his birth, how is that possible?

Jesus answered, neither hath this man sinned, nor his parents: but that the works of God should be made manifest in him." We understand this answer but what is not said speaks loudly. Jesus could have said, what a foolish question. How can he sin before he's born, he didn't exist. Or did he?

We're having fun reviewing scripture, right? So why stop now? Take a look at Matt. 13:10, 11 "And the disciples came, and said unto Him, Why speakest Thou unto them in parables?" "He answered and said unto them, because it is given unto you to know the mysteries of the kingdom of heaven, but to them it is not given." Why, would group of people not be given to understand? If not, why bother to speak to them at all? This baffled me for years and must admit, upset me. Was this fair?

Now I could ask you to read Matt.13:24 through 30 but for time and scrutiny, allow me to quote it. "Another parable put He forth unto them, saying, the kingdom of heaven is likened unto a man which sowed good seed in his field: But while he slept, his enemy came and sowed tares among the wheat, and went his way. But when the blade was sprung up, and brought forth fruit, then appeared the tares also." "From whence then hath it tares?" He said unto them, an enemy hath done this." The servants said unto him, "Wilt thou then we go and gather them up?" But he said, "Nay; lest while ye gather up the tares, ye root up also the wheat with them. Let both grow together until the harvest: and in the time of harvest I will say to the reapers, Gather ye together first the tares, and bind them in bundles to burn them: But gather the wheat into my barn."

Before telling this parable Jesus explained, " because they seeing see not; and hearing they hear not, neither do they understand." He went on to say, "If they did, and converted, He would heal them." Jesus told the disciples that their eyes could see and their ears could hear. We're not talking physical here, it's spiritual or by their spirit. Remember, God is spirit and must be worshiped in spirit.

This parable of the "tares" is practically self-explanatory. The sower is God, the field is the world, and the enemy is the evil one (Satan). What is a tare? In the Greek it's -zizanion (*dziz-an'-ee-on)* meaning - false grain. Tears are plants that look like twins to the wheat plant. The difference: when the plants begin to fruit the grain of the tare is dark, almost black (and is poisonous). Until the grain appeared, the tares were undetectable.

What is being conveyed here? Precisely the matter we've been discussing: Nephilim-Hybrids.

Also the Kenites, but that is a road I'll not go down now; you're probably having trouble keeping it between the ditches as it is.

These hybrids show up as myths and legends in almost every culture in history. But it's the scripture that tells the real (behind the scenes) story. The secret or mystery mentioned throughout the bible.

You know, a lot of scripture is parable like or metaphoric, we're not going to understand unless we can spiritually discern it. Yet it's there for us. "Study to show thyself approved unto God, a workman that needeth not to be ashamed, rightly dividing (divining) the word of truth." 2nd Tim. 2:15 Dividing - orthotomeo (*or-thot-om-eh'-or*) to dissect (expound) correctly (*the divine message*) There are hundreds of scriptures that give clues or references to "The Mystery of God." We have reviewed a few of them. Therefore, keeping in mind all that's been said thus far; let me tell a story...

Chapter VII

The Egg Hunt

A man in the church, once spoke to me about having an Easter egg hunt. "AT THE CHURCH?!" I replied. "Look if you want to have an egg hunt at your house, fine. Maybe if you ask real nice I might even help you hide 'em, but a church sanctioned Easter egg hunt. I'll fight you over it!" Having shared that, let me tell you about an egg hunt many years ago. It must have been about 1950, I was around three at the time, in my sage field.

The church we (my family) attended was two or three blocks from granddads property. "Pap" was gracious in letting them have the egg hunt in his field. Dozens of kids, with frilly baskets and colored eggs, scurried across the field. I on the other hand, literally being held by the hand, had no eggs in my basket.

This woman holding my hand, can't recall who she was, a sitter, friend, perhaps a Sunday school teacher. Whoever she was began to whisper saying "psst-look here" or "there." Hey! This was alright, my basket was no longer empty. After a while she whispered "look". Standing with her heels together and her feet apart, said "dig." Quickly I was down on my knees digging leaves from a hole in the ground at her feet. To my surprise this hole reviled the biggest egg I'd ever seen. The PRIZE EGG! This magnificent ostrich egg was colored gold and had rhinestones running in two directions forming a cross. Wow, can you imagine? This little kid, that big egg, the excitement! Well that was a long time ago. What I do remember was the prize, a chocolate bunny, yum.

It's for the children they often say. What harm is there in Easter egg hunts? In and of itself nothing, but when it's made to appear to be part of Passover or THE RESURECTION, it's an abomination! The only time the word Easter appears in the bible is Acts 12:4 and it is mistranslated. The word in the Greek text is pascha pronounced - (*pas'-khah*) meaning Passover. The word Easter comes from Easter (a.k.a. Easter) a fertility goddess of spring. Eostre from which the word estrogen is derived.

Also the bunny is a symbol of —-Oh, well enough of that. Suffice to say I'm a'gn it!

Where was I? Oh yeah, the Sunday school egg hunt. I got the prize! Why? I found the prize egg fair and square-right? What is the meaning of the word fair? We know the location was revealed to me by the aforementioned mystery woman. Surely there was a prior relationship. Did she say to herself, there's a cute kid; I'll show him the prize egg? I think not, there had to be a prior relationship. Was it fair to the other children? Had they stumbled along and found it, would they have gotten the prize? Ponder these questions as we continue our journey.

Chapter VIII

The Fall

"I will open my mouth in parables; I will utter things which have been kept secret from the foundation of the world." Matt. 13:35

There was a time, before the *overthrow,* or the *katabole,* when Lucifer the anointed cherub, walked amid the fiery stones. He became prideful in his position and was able to convince a third of the "Sons of God" to rebel.

Can you imagine, Lucifer the light bearer, the morning star, rebelling against God? The seductive power of Satan is -is unexplainable. Which is why Eve was no match for him. But I'm getting ahead of the story.

Yet, let me get personal for just a moment. A while back I was brushing my granddaughter's hair. Usually a horrific ordeal, this time though she was quite talkative. "Pa", she said "does the devil love us? "No dear "I replied "He just tries to make us think he does." (Sarah, was about three years old) Jumping to her feet, whirling around, with hands on her hips. Exclaimed "Yes!" And I don't know why I listen to him." I began to tell her how we should listen to the Lord, believe in and trust Him. And To be good so we can be with Him when we die, unlike bad people. "What about me?" she said "I'm bad." Ready to negate her statement, being checked simply replied "Oh, you are?" "Yes" she began "I be mean, I pitch fits, I choke..." Choking her playmates, when they fought, was a practice she had been disciplined more than once. The child was listing her sins! She had acknowledged she was a sinner. She confessed her sin. A place we must all come to.

"Sarah!" "If you ask the Lord to forgive you He will. Then ask Him to come into your heart and be your Savoir." Immediately she was on her knees. I can hear you- "she was too young." Point being, here was a babe fresh from the Kingdom. Aware of her state in this world and desiring to solidify her standing.

Back to the story. Satan and his followers of course were overthrown, praise the Lord! Father had the right to destroy them, I know I probably would have. They were His children! He created them, but could He trust them? He had to prove who loved Him, not to Himself, to all concerned.

Have you ever heard of a judge sentencing a youth to military service? Saying "If you successfully complete your tour, the charges will be dropped. This is kind of what the Lord did, but not so simply. Remember we discussed Gen. 1:26, God said "Let *us* make man in *our* image, after *our* likeness..." Father is talking to His children, telling them how He's going to handle this. His plan of redemption included the flesh, the "Sons of God" were to put on and be clothed with flesh.

Up to this point there was no such thing as woman, hence *Sons of God.* Woman was unique in God's plan. She (Eve) would become, umbilical cord to umbilical cord, the Mother of all living. This new world would have only one legitimate entry (doorway): the womb. They that would come any other way, "the same is a thief and a robber." John 10:1

Not only were the rebellious children required to pass through the flesh. Those that stood with Father, also became sojourners in the flesh. Now the best part of the plan; God Himself would take on flesh. To become *Theanthrops = The God Man. (in the fullness of time)*

There was some judging going on at this time too. Satan became the son of perdition; the only one (so far) sentenced to death. No redemption! Others were listed in The Book of Life. Christ said "Lo, I come in the volume of the book it is written of me", Heb. 10:7 (at the head of the list) "For whom He did foreknow, He also did predestinate to be conformed to the image of His Son, that He might be the firstborn among many brethren."

And there was a group of rebellious spirits that left their principality with Father, stepping out of their habitation, becoming thieves and robbers. Not wanting to be born from above. (See John 3:3) As previously stated; they didn't want to be born of woman, they wanted to seduce woman.

Satan had been condemned to death; a real "dead man walking." He had nothing to lose (though he thinks he can win in the end) and sent forth these fallen ones to seduce woman, as he had seduced Eve in the garden. Eve said " The serpent (*nachash=shining one*) beguiled me..." Beguiled? It means to wholly seduce. Does anyone believe the serpent was a snake? Fasten your seatbelt we've turned down that road!

What was the real sin in the Garden? Did Eve eat an apple (or some fruit) to cause the downfall of mankind?

"Now the serpent was more *subtle* than any *beast* of the field, which the Lord God had made." Gen. 3:1. We've discussed the meaning of the word serpent *nachash- shining one.* Here was an angelic being (not a snake) standing before Eve. Yes! She was impressed with this god-like creature and yes, she listened to him. The old-English word *beast* here means living creature, not a snake or ox as one may envision being of the field. The field being the world, metaphorically speaking through out scripture. The word subtle of course means wise. This being was the wisest of any the Lord God had made. Yea, hath God said, "Ye shall not eat of every tree of the garden?" quoted Satan.

"And the woman said unto the serpent, we may eat of the fruit of the trees of the garden: but of the fruit of the tree which is in the midst of the garden, God hath said, ye shall not eat of it, neither shall ye touch it, lest ye die." Gen. 3:3 Some say Eve added the part about not touching it. True, that is not what God told Adam, but who knows what He told Eve? And the serpent said unto the woman, "Ye shall not surely die" Gen. 3:4 "For God doth know that in the day ye eat thereof, then your eyes shall be opened, and ye shall be as gods, knowing good and evil."

" And when the woman saw that the tree was good for food, and that it was pleasant to the eyes, and a tree to be desired to make one wise, she took of the fruit thereof, and did eat, and gave also unto her husband with her; and he did eat", partake. This word tree-*athes*=firmness or backbone. Is there any doubt who this tree was? You know there was another tree in the garden, The Tree of Life. We have no problem understanding who this Tree is, that gives eternal life, and it is Christ. (The pre-incarnate Christ)

So of course the tree of knowledge of good and evil was the devil or satan.

Let's back-up to Eve, she said "...neither shall ye touch it." The word touch in this verse is naga-*naw-gah,* to lay the hand upon, to lie with a woman. Remember how in verse 6 she is lusting after the tree, it was pleasant to the eyes, and to be desired to make one wise, desires of the flesh. Gen. 3:13 says "And the Lord God said unto the woman, "What is this that thou hast done? And the woman said. "The serpent *beguiled* me..."

Beguiled in the Hebrew nasha *naw-shaw* meaning to seduce. The word in the Greek as used in

2 Cor. 11:3 "...as the serpent beguiled Eve..." is exapato *ex-ap-at-ah-o,* to wholly seduce. If we look at the context of 2 Cor.11:3 back up to verse 1 which reads "... Would to God ye could bear with me a little in my folly: and indeed bear with me." The writer here is saying, I may sound a little reckless, but I'm speaking morally, so listen and understand what I'm saying.

Continuing with verse 2 "For I am jealous over you with Godly jealousy: for I have espoused you to one husband, that I may present you a chaste virgin to Christ." 3 "But I fear, least by any means, as the serpent beguiled Eve through his subtlety, so your minds should be corrupted from the simplicity that is Christ."

Ok, so if you are no longer chaste, you have gone a whoring after the serpent, (or tree). Whoring, that's an interesting word, in the Hebrew it's zanah *zaw-naw* to commit adultery. Is there any question what Eve did?

Now the scripture says: "...she took of the fruit thereof, and did eat, and gave also unto her husband with her; and he did eat." He was with her! What exactly Adam did is not clear. Did satan appear as a woman? Was the act simply a menageatrois or was Adam's sin partaking of his wife, therefore partaking of her sin? (A side note here; if you vote for a candidate (seriously support) you become a partaker of their sin. (Known sin)

Alright, let's return to Gen. 3:13 "And the Lord God said unto the woman: What is that thou hast done? He said to the serpent (satan) verse 15 "And I will put enmity between thee and the woman, and between thy seed and her seed; It shall bruise thy head, and thou shall bruise His heel."

Chapter IX

Questions

We've all asked ourselves, why am I here and where did I come from? Do you know the answers?

People will often say "where is that in the bible? They want chapter and verse. Sometimes I'm able to quote chapter and verse. Other times say in this book and verse, also go to this other book verse 3&4 etc. Some will say I don't see it. Again, "study to show thyself approved unto God, a workman that needeth not to be ashamed, rightly dividing the word of truth." 2 Tim. 2:15 Scripture at times must be divinely interpreted.

The bible is about one family, from Adam to Abraham to Jesus. There is a red thread that runs through all of scripture. That thread is Christ! Let me say this and move on.

It's like a Christmas wreath, one may say, that's a lovely wreath where did you get it? "In the forest" I reply. Where in the forest" they say. "Well the twigs and pine cones, on the ground, the fir and pine branches, on their respective trees." "The holly berries and branches from the holly bush." "It's quite lovely, is it not?"

Chapter X

Understanding

Not only did we come to this realm to die but to find Christ! Trying to understand what father God was doing to resolve the katabole situation. The rebellious children (sons of God) had to be punished. If in God's place, I would have probably destroyed them. But the Lord loved His children; and being God had to be fair and just! As previously stated "And God said let us make man (flesh) in our image, after our likeness", Gen. 1:26. Thus the sons of God had to become flesh. To be born of woman!

The non-rebellious were to become flesh as well. To be called the Zadok (Elect). These elect do not have free will! Thus may be used by God to effect His will and to help the non-elect find Christ. Example; pharaoh of Egypt. Seven times God hardened pharaoh's heart. (So apparently the Lord violated pharaoh's free will) Exodus 9:16 "...for this cause have I raised thee up, for to show in thee my power, and that my name may be declared throughout all the earth." Pharaoh one of God's elect? I think so. Matt. 7:1 "Judge not, that you be not judged..." We're talking "salvation." To judge someone's salvation is wrong. To do so may be judging God's Elect. As the scripture says "all Israel shall be saved."

"For whom He did foreknow; He also did predestinate to be conformed to the image of His son, that He might be the firstborn among many brethren." God Himself would take on flesh; to become Theanthropos, The God Man. "Moreover whom He did predestinate, Them He also called: and whom He called, them He also justified: and whom He justified, them He also glorified", Romans 8:30. The word justified here means to judge. Some of us came into this world pre-judged; with a golden ticket. (Remember Willy Wonka and the Chocolate Factory.) Pun intended!

Understanding this life (existence), understanding where we came from and why we're here, knowing we have a history with our heavenly Father, believing the roots of our family tree run through eternity and aware that our presence in this dimension is because of the overthrow of satan (the katabole), we came here to die and to find Christ! (Not in that order)

I believe the Lord puts every child in the family, which gives them the best chance to make it out of here! (to glory) And the Elect in our lives, lead guide and direct us. Pointing the way to Christ! My mother and my paternal grandmother were two such people. Even homes that are unloving and neglectful; God knows what He is doing! Being in this realm is all part of punishment and or redemption. Some folks come into this world with a lot of baggage. Some come kicking and screaming: remember Esau?

Do you recall the story of the egg hunt? My grandfather's field, all the children? The prize Egg? My telling of The Egg Hunt is a true story.

However it's like a parable or a metaphor. Both parables and metaphors have hidden meanings. A parable is longer and uses a story to convey a deeper message. Metaphors are typically shorter and refer to one subject, while the actual subject is something else entirely. Call it what you will, here's the scoop: The field is the world, the children are the souls that came into this realm. And the Prize

Egg is Jesus the Christ! Not to forget the mystery woman, she represents God's Elect.

We previously discussed said mystery woman. Whether or not it was fair for her to show me the location of the prize egg. Again, understanding where we came from and why we're here. Metaphorically: Yes!

God already knows our fate. However, by having lived in this realm we will understand our punishment or reward is just! What are our options? You know hell was made for the devil and his angels, Matt. 25:41. Satan will not be ruling in hell, but cast into the fire! Those who reject Christ will be cast into the lake of fire! Those who accept Him will receive everlasting life in Heaven! Ponder these things as we continue our journey toward understanding Matthew 7:21.

Chapter XI

Truth

"Wherefore by their fruits ye shall know them. Not everyone that sayeth unto me, Lord, Lord, shall enter into the kingdom of heaven; but he that doeth the will of my Father which is in heaven. Many will say to me in that day, Lord, Lord, have we not prophesied in thy name? And in thy name have cast out devils? And in thy name done many wonderful works? And will I profess unto them, I NEVER KNEW YOU: depart from me, ye that work iniquity." Matt. 7:20-23

Who is the Lord talking to? Obviously, people who think they are religious. In today's vernacular-Christians, People that believe they are "in" with God. Jesus' words sound rough and jarring to the senses. However they are Truth!

I know you love it, so let's go to our word definitions. The Lord said "I never knew you." The word knew is *ginosko* in the Greek. Meaning to know absolutely-to feel. In the Hebrew it is *yada* to lie by man. "And Cain knew his wife; and she conceived, and bare Enoch..." So what is Jesus saying "I never knew you?" The word knew means to touch, to feel and to lie with man, to know absolutely. In Cain's case we're talking carnal knowledge (sex). Is this what the Lord is saying? Not to be vulgar or profane, but yes! Spiritual intercourse or Divine Intimacy!

The book of Acts tells of the seven sons of Sceva who tried to cast out evil spirits. Saying "We adjure you by Jesus whom Paul preacheth" "And the evil spirit answered and said Jesus I know and Paul I know; but who are you?" Then the evil spirit jumped on them, beat them, so they fled out of the house naked and wounded. ref. from Acts 19:13 thru 16. Some folks have heard about Jesus, read about Jesus and even prays to Jesus. But they don't know Jesus, thus their religion is in vain.

Personally I believe 75% of the back sides that warm the pews on Sunday will split hell wide-open! They have a knowledge of Christ but not a real relationship. I've often said "going to church will not make you a Christian, any more than going to McDonald's will make you a Big Mac! Now that I've had my funny. Let me say church attendance can and often does lead to salvation.

Frequently I'll meet people at a corner store; begging or bumming. Most of the time it's the same story; "I'm out of gas, my car is up on the interstate." When I offer to take them to their car, the story changes. Questioning, "are you a Christian do you know the Lord? Almost always the answer is yes. Quizzing them further "so what does that make you?" Getting all kinds of response, finally I'll say "it makes you a child of the King!" "And if you are a child of the king, what are you doing out here begging?" "Something is wrong with that relationship!"

Relationship, an intimate relationship is what it's all about. Not I think it so, I believe it so, or to work it up in one's mind. (See ch.2-Faith) If you're having intercourse with someone, odds are you know that person VERY WELL! You have an INTIMATE RELATIONSHIP! (If you're Not married; you're living in SIN, and don't tell me you're married in the eyes of God, He's Not smiling!)

"And that not of yourselves; it is the gift of God: Not of works, least any man should boast..." Created in Christ unto good works, which God hath before ordained..." Eph. 9:10 Folks; its not us! We cannot think ourselves saved, wish or claim ourselves so. Even our righteous acts will not tip the scale. It's God that does the calling! "For many are called, but few are chosen." Matt. 22:14 what does that mean? It means many are invited but only a few make the cut! Do you recall the song "Ballad of The Green Beret?" And the line "one hundred men will test today but only three win the Green Beret" 2 Peter 3:9 says in part, "...not willing that any should perish, but all should come to repentance." It's God's desire that all should come (invited) to Christ and not suffer damnation.

However "Enter ye in the strait gate: for wide is the gate, and broad is the way, that leadeth to destruction, and many there be which go in thereat: because strait is the gate, and narrow is the way, which leadeth unto life, and few there be that find it." Matt. 7:13-14. Dear one, it's because of your pre-existence or pre-mortal existence, that the Holy Spirit can draw you to Himself!

We talked about the elect and the non-elect. If you are of the elect; God's call is on your life! (The Golden Ticket) Those of the non-elect; the Holy Spirit may draw you to Himself! Again, the elect in your life will point you to Jesus, if you hear the call in your spirit, seek Him.

I could ask you to look-up John 14, maybe you would, maybe not. Allow me to tell you about John 14, not verbatim perhaps. But it's hard not to quote.

Jesus told His disciples: you believe in God, then believe in Me. My Father's house has many rooms. I go to prepare a place for you. And I will come again and receive you, that where I am you may be also. Where I go you know, and the way you know. Thomas said we don't know where you're going, how can we know the way? Jesus said I am the way, the truth and the life: no man can come to the Father but by me. If you have known me, you should know my Father too. Henceforth you know Him and have seen Him. Philip said show us the Father and it will be sufficient for us. Jesus said have I been so long time with you, that you don't know me, Philip? He said the Father is in me and I in the Father. The Father and I are one! Jesus is God. Creator God took on flesh to become the Sacrificial Lamb! He and only He could make The Sacrifice; wrap your mind around that!

John 14:15 says "If you love me keep my commandments." "And those that love me not keepeth not my sayings". Children, it's the relationship! The intimate relationship you have with your spouse, is because of love. When you love someone you respect them. Not in any way do you want to bring shame or disrespect. If we are professing Christ and not keeping His commandments. We are bringing shame and disrespect into the relationship. One needs to rethink that relationship! If you are relying on baptism, a so called prayer, or something preacher so and so said. You may be a victim of easy believeism. I know you've been told- once saved always saved. And if a real change actually took place. Maybe so?

Years ago when I was trying to quit smoking. (Quit in 86) Talking to a friend, I said why don't God take these cigarettes away from me? He said what do you want Him to do? Smack them out of your mouth! You must lay them down!

My friend was right, I had to lay them down! When God calls, speaks and encourages; we must step out. Step out in "faith". Not I think it so, or I hope it so! (see ch. 2) " Faith comes by hearing and hearing by the Word of God." Romans 10:17 When we " hear" from God, trust what He said. So knowing His will: I laid them down. Yes, I was tempted to pick them up again. But didn't want to disappoint my Lord! Dear one, are you seeing, are you about to understand?

Chapter XII

Salvation

Adam and Eve sinned when they partook of what God had forbidden. What really took place in the garden? (See ch.8) God Himself killed an animal(s) to make coats of skin to cover them. The Lord sacrificed an animal; shed its blood to cover their sin. From the beginning, Father has said the payment for sin is death: and so blood must be shed to cover sin! "For the life of a creature is in the blood, and I have given it to you to make atonement for yourselves on the altar, it is the blood that makes atonement for one's life." Leviticus 17:11 "In fact, the law requires that nearly everything be cleansed with blood, and without the shedding of blood there is no forgiveness" Hebrews 9:22

Imagine one innocent being shedding its blood in place of the sinner's. The sacrificing of bulls and lambs for the sins of each person, was a temporary fix. Because the next year another animal would have to be sacrificed for the same person. "For it is impossible for the blood of bulls and goats to take away sins. Hebrews 10:4 Thus a human was needed to die for human's sin! However humans since Adam are sinful. To do away with bulls, goats and lambs; a sinless human must be sacrificed. How would that be possible? God Himself became a man: Jesus! Thus when one accepts Jesus they are covered by HIS blood!! Covered; once and for all!

Taking a closer look at the animal sacrifice; Adam and Eve recognized their mortality. Remembering; God had said they would surely die. (If they partook of the forbidden tree) Knowing they were walking in the shadow of death! As Andrious Valevicius once said "A revolution has occurred: life used to be the fundamental principle of human existence but now it has been clothed by mortality. Death has gained the advance, and life which used to unfold unthreatened, has been transformed into a fight for survival" All the result of sin.

The theme of pre-judgement grace runs throughout Scripture. Adam and Eve were covered prior to being cast out of the garden. Cain was given a mark before being exiled. God gave a covenant before the flood and we could speak of Joseph's coat (covering). Point being man is inadequate when it comes to covering his sin. (The fig leaves) All this Grace points to the coming Christ. Which is the epitome of Grace. God's unmerited favor!

What have you done with Jesus? Most of us have heard about Jesus. We've heard bible stories, friends and acquaintances may have spoken the name of Jesus. Maybe we've been exposed to Jesus by television or some preacher. So what have you done with this knowledge? Tucked it somewhere deep in the canyons of your mind? Maybe filed it under "I'll think about that one day".

My father was a brilliant man. (See ch.4) I talked to him often about Jesus. One day I poured my heart out to him about accepting Christ! My father was not a well man; he had congestive heart failure along with kidney problems. Thus he was forced to drag a catheter bag everywhere he went. Once, while on the back deck with him, I said "Dad what have you done with Jesus?" "Let's go back in the house" he replied, abruptly ending the conversation. A few days later my mother called to say dad had passed away. Going to him, I found he was sitting in his easy chair, looking like he was sleeping. Taking his face in my hands and saying

"Dad why didn't you listen? As I spoke those words, it was like a choir began to sing: "Turn your eyes upon Jesus, look full in HIS wonderful face and the things of earth will grow strangely dim in the light of His glory and grace" Was the Lord saying "don't concern yourself with that now, focus on Me"? Could be, it seemed to help at the moment.

Many of us have heard of Jesus. Once learning of Jesus, what do we do with this knowledge? We are profoundly responsible; seeing as it's one of the main reasons we are here/to find our redeemer! A lot of folks think no more about it. Some say; yeah I want that and claim it. Therefore going through life believing they have an "in" with Christ. However not being committed! And some think they are committed but not keeping His commandments.

I challenge you: walk-up to a random stranger. "Do you know the Lord, are you a Christian? Ninety-nine percent will say yes! Can this be true? If so preaching is vain. The Lord said "Go ye into all the world and preach the gospel to every creature". It would appear our job is done here! However ungodliness abounds!

Chapter XIII

Commitment

Every football season, we hear of young men signing a letter of commitment to a certain college. Some of these young men will de-commit. What? How can one de-commit? Just what is the meaning of commitment? The Webster's definition-an agreement or pledge to do something. An obligation, a promise. A pledge is a solemn promise- a thing given as security for the fulfillment of a contract or the payment; liable to forfeiture in the event of failure.

Commitment is a very serious matter. And should not be entered into lightly. Breaking a commitment could have dire consequences. Seeing a pledge may be liable to forfeiture. Forfeiture of what? That which is pledged!

What has all of this to do with salvation? Previously we discussed; the Lord does the calling. Once you realize you are a sinner and moved to do something about it. Chances are you have been called! Knowing and believing the sacrifice Jesus made for you. You must invite Him into your life and commit your life to HIM! "And I give them eternal life, and they shall never perish; neither shall anyone snatch them out of my hand." John 10:28

Dear one make your calling and your election sure! "According as His divine power hath given unto us all things that pertain unto life and godliness, through the knowledge of Him that has called us to glory and virtue. Whereby are given unto us exceeding great and precious promises: that by these ye might be partakers of the divine nature, having escaped the corruption that is in the world through lust. And beside this, giving all diligence, add to your faith virtue; and to virtue knowledge; and to knowledge temperance and to temperance patience; and to patience godliness; and to godliness brotherly kindness; and to brotherly kindness charity.

For if these things be in you, and abound they make you that ye shall neither be barren nor unfruitful in the knowledge of our Lord Jesus

Christ. But he that lacketh these things is blind, and cannot see afar off, and hath forgotten that he was purged from his old sins. Wherefore the rather, brethren, give diligence to make your calling and election sure: for if ye do these things, ye shall never fall."

2Peter 1:3-10

As a rule, I generally don't like to copy so much scripture. However it seemed necessary for context.

The idea of commitment has a permanence about it. It's not something to change your mind about. So to commit one's life to Christ, is to pledge your life! Commitment in essence means: even if I have to Die! If this is not your relationship with Jesus Christ: Your religion is in vain!!

"In everything give thanks. For this is the will of God in Christ Jesus concerning you." 1 Thess. 5:18 "This" means whatever is going on in your life! Trust Him! Involve Him in every aspect of your life! It may sound silly; I once told my son "ask the Lord which soft drink to take from the cooler"! He wants to be involved; He wants that intimate relationship. Dear one, do things, not because they're easy or convenient, but because they are right! Rules matter, especially His commandments.

We can't be truly righteous "...all our righteousness are as filthy rags" Isaiah 64:6 But we must strive to be a good and faithful servant!

Those of you who are married understand; that you are not to bring shame or disgrace into the relationship. Nor are you to be unfaithful. Because you know in doing so could have dire consequences. Even the removal of you from the relationship!

Dear one if you haven't given your life to Jesus Christ: don't let another day dawn! "Today if ye hear His voice, harden not your hearts, as in the provocation. For some, when they had heard, did provoke: howbeit not all that came out of Egypt by Moses. But with whom was he grieved forty years? Was it not with them that had sinned, whose carcasses fell in the wilderness?" Hebrews 3:15-17

"Be not deceived: neither fornicators, nor idolaters, nor adulterers, nor effeminate, nor abusers of themselves with mankind, nor thieves, nor covetous, nor drunkards, nor revilers, nor extortioners, shall inherit the kingdom of God." And such were some of you: but ye are washed, but ye are sanctified, but ye are justified in the name of the Lord Jesus, and by the Spirit of God." 1Cor.6:9-11

Beloved, don't be deceived in your religion (belief). Strive for that spiritual intimate relationship with God through Jesus Christ! If you have heard Him call, if you have felt the tug on your heart; answer. If your name is called your presence is required! Enter into His presence.

I Struggle every day to be a faithful servant. Seeing myself falling short, fearfully maneuvering through life. Yet confident and trusting His Blood, His Sacrifice are sufficient for my salvation! Knowing one day I shall be with Him in paradise!

Dear one, strive to make your calling and election Sure! Don't be one who thinks they have an "in" with God; A "Golden ticket." My prayer is, you never hear- "Away from me, you evildoer, I NEVER KNEW YOU"

Having read these few words of mine, understand. YOU ARE WITHOUT EXCUSE!